The Culture of Agency

The Culture of Agency

Taking your insurance agency to the next level by creating and fostering your unique, dynamic culture

Ulyanna Chung

Publisher: Ulyanna Chung
Cover and design by Darryl Martin

ISBN 978-0-578-85192-1

Introduction

I don't know one person who says they wanted to be an insurance agent when they grew up. It's something that most of us "fell into." Maybe our first job was in an agent's office, or we had family members who were in insurance. It also could be that we wanted to own a business, and this was an opportunity. This is my journey into the wonderful field of insurance.

I was born into a lower-middle class Korean immigrant family. My parents valued education and excellence – think Asian "tiger mom." Growing up, my parents stressed doing your best – giving it your all, and I tried to live up to those values. I was an excellent student and went to one of the top universities in the country, UCLA (Go Bruins!).

I tell this next story, even though my mother completely denies it, because it illustrates my childhood. I was pre-med at UCLA and taking an organic chemistry class. This was one of the hardest classes at one of the hardest universities. There were 400 top students, and I got the third highest grade in the class. Seriously, I wanted to frame that grade. When I told my mother about it, her response was, "why were you not first or second?" Don't get me wrong - my parents are loving people, but they were "pushers." You push to be the best, to succeed, to win.

I graduated from UCLA with honors and was accepted into medical school. At my interview, the dean of admissions of the medical school asked me if I really wanted to be a doctor, or if, perhaps, it was the dream of my parents. At the time, I gave a brilliant answer of how this was my "dream and passion." But, when I got home, I began to question my own response and started looking at different possible options.

At the time, the job center at UCLA had a posting for the U.S. Customs Service. I applied on a whim. Seriously, I should not have been hired! I had no idea of the requirements of the job. The interviewer asked me a scenario-based question, "What would you do if someone became belligerent and violent at the airport?" My response, "Call the police!" Ummmm, you ARE the police! (Oh, geeze!) Although I should not have been hired for the position, law enforcement came extremely easy to me. I got to carry and shoot a gun and tell people what to do! It was a natural fit. While I was in training at the Federal Law Enforcement Training Center, I got my acceptance letter into medical school. I truly believe that life is about the choices we make, and I wonder how my life would have turned out if I had gone to medical school as originally planned.

Although I had no idea about the job requirements, I excelled at Customs. I earned expert shooter awards and received two Commissioner's Awards in my short four years with the Agency. I was also accepted into the Federal Executive Program which develops the future executive leaders in federal service. Then 9/11 happened! Although I was on the fast track with Customs, I decided to apply for the Federal Air Marshal Program – I was driven toward adventure. During my second time at the Federal Law Enforcement Training Center, I met my husband. We were friends until we weren't – wink wink!

I tell everyone that the Air Marshal position is the best job for a single person, but my then-boyfriend (future husband) and I were starting to get serious. We talked about getting married and starting a family, which would have been way too hard with both parents traveling all over the world. At the time, we had bought our first house, and I was shopping for insurance. I walked into our local neighborhood insurance office and met Amber Aiello.

I mentioned that I was thinking of making a career change. She explained to me the benefits of owning your own insurance agency. Less than one year later, I opened the doors to my agency. This was the first time in my professional career that I did not excel naturally. Not only did I have to make sales, I needed to lead people. I had to motivate and inspire my staff, and I was lost. I knew the value of hard work, so I managed to have years of growth and success due to many long, long hours. However, that type of work level was not sustainable in the long run. I would burn out and take my foot off the gas pedal, and then, sure enough, I would have a slump year. I could see the negative impact on my business, so I would once again start the long hours. It was an eleven year roller coaster of business highs and business lows.

I knew that something needed to change. The roller coaster was emotionally and mentally draining. I hired a business coach who was all about "systems." She advocated that there needed to be clarity and consistency for employees. There was a system for everything. I spent the next year building and implementing my business systems, and I was able to see improvement in production, but not at the level I had hoped for.

About that time, I was visiting with a colleague, Eric Moreno, who was experiencing success in his agency. I showed him my systems, and he was amazed. He said that my employees had to suck if they couldn't excel in my office. Now that was a serious statement, and I was a little shocked. Yes, I agreed that some of my employees were not great, but some of my employees were amazing. The whole team didn't "suck."

At the same time, one of my former employees, Jason Paszek, had opened his agency and was having enormous success. I was telling my husband that although

I was extremely proud of my former employee, his performance was unfortunately making me feel like a loser. My husband asked me what I thought Jason was doing differently. I was joking, but I said, "I don't know." I was smarter, funnier, and cuter than Jason - what was the deal? I took some time to think about it. My former employee, Jason, was one of the most disciplined people I know. I, on the other hand - I am the ultimate dreamer. I tell my friends, "this week, I am really into …". I say, "this week," because next week, it will be a different passion.

These two incidents created a shift in my thinking. I had created these systems in my office, and I expected huge success, because I expected my employees to change with the systems – but I hadn't changed. I never worked on myself as a person or a leader. What is that famous quote from Ghandi, "*Be the change you want to see in the world.*"

I read an amazing quote, "*Let your business work on you.*" I thought about all my career choices and why I opened my business. Doctor, law enforcement officer, and Insurance agent – all these career choices were about helping people. At the time, I already had a personal vision statement that was, "Be the best version of myself for my family, friends, team, and community," but I did not have a vision statement for my agency. I thought about it. I thought about why I started this business and about my values. My agency "vision statement" became, "*Bee a difference in the lives of the people on my team, my agency, and my community.*" It is spelled "bee" - this is not a typo. Our mascot became the "bee." I know! Super cheesy!

From this vision statement, my team and I came up with values and a mission statement. We worked on our communication skills and developed a culture of excellence and personal development in my agency. I worked on my leadership skills and brought those skills to my team. We worked on creating a culture that valued ownership, accountability, and accomplishments. What we were inadvertently doing was creating a culture that had goals, systems, and just plain fun. That's when we started seeing success through our joint achievements.

It didn't happen overnight. This was a two-to-three-year process. There were bumps in the road, and it's still not perfect. We work daily to make sure that we continue the culture. Just because you achieve your goal weight doesn't mean you should stop working out and eating right. It's the daily choices that help us achieve our goals.

Whether you know it or not, **YOU** have a "culture" in **YOUR** agency. It can be positive or negative - but, is it the culture you want? Let's get started on creating an amazing culture that will enable you to have a consistently successful agency that produces year after year– the amazing culture of **YOUR** dreams!

Table of Contents

Culture

You may not think you have an "agency culture" – but you do. It is reflected by the beliefs and behaviors of you, the agency owner, and by your team members. It may not be clearly defined, but it is reflected in the operations of your agency, from who you hire, how your team is trained, customer service, and agency production and growth.

For example, there are highly successful agencies that are transactional, and there are highly successful agencies are that more relationship based. Some agencies operate as a call center, and some agencies are more localized neighborhood agencies. That is the culture of those agencies. Even without it being clearly defined, we would be able to easily identity these cultures. There are also positive and negative transactional agency cultures, and there are positive and negative relationship-based cultures.

Culture is important to your agency because it sets the tone for everything. Culture influences production performance, team engagement, and recruitment and retention of team and customers. Research by Gallup's *State of the American Workplace* has shown that 51% of employees report not being engaged in their job. When employees are engaged, absenteeism decreases by 41%; turnover lowers by 24%; and productivity is increased by 17%.

The culture creates the work environment in your office for your team. Is it fun to come to work every day, or is it a chore? Do your team members get along and communicate, or is it a toxic environment? This translates to all aspects of your business. If your culture is not a positive one, then you and your team members are not happy. If you, the agent, are unhappy and your office culture is negative, it will slowly infect your team, due to a lack of training, criticisms of team members, and the lack of praise. If they are unhappy, it affects their motivation for sales, the type of service they provide to your customers, and their longevity in your agency. The culture creates the environment that your customers experience. When customers walk in, are they greeted in a friendly, inviting fashion, or are team members glued to their desks?

If you have a negative culture, you can still have growth and success in your agency. In fact, you can have a highly profitable and producing agency, but still have a negative culture. That being said, you may ask, "Why is culture important, if my agency is rocking it?" The answer is that your agency will be a roller coaster ride in production and/or emotional stability. There will be high highs and low lows. Your agency will lack consistency. You may have great years or horrible years, but there will always be numerous fires to put out. It will feel like there is some big issue with a team member or with a client every single day. You will also have constant turnover of your team, and hiring and training new team members is a long and expensive journey.

A negative culture will always create an unhealthy environment in a small insurance agency (less than 25 team members). We sometimes spend more time with our co-workers than our families. Just like our families, we may like and care for our co-workers, but they can annoy or just plain infuriate us. When you have a negative culture in an office, it will feel like high school - we all like each other in a group, but when a person leaves, we gossip behind their back. There is a lot of gossiping, griping, and fighting. As the owner of your agency, are you constantly playing mediator between your team members? This is an example of the effects of a negative culture.

Yet, having a positive culture doesn't make everything perfect. Come on! We can all sit around the campfire singing "kumbaya," but at the end of the day, we are a sales organization. We need to produce. A positive culture can create an environment where consistency is the key, where everyone on the team focuses on making it work in a positive and ethical way; and where everyone on the team is accountable.

Types of Culture

The three cultures are the "**systems culture**," the "**people culture**," and the "**competition culture**."

The "**systems culture**" is a control culture. The workplace is more formal and structured. Procedures, formal rules, efficiency, and organization are highly valued. There is emphasis on details and the long-term goal is stability. In this culture, the agency can get stuck in the systems and reports. The owner is probably an analytical and somewhat controlling person. He/she will analyze every report, and there is a system for everything, which can result in "paralysis by analysis." The systems are all there, In the small insurance agency (less than 25 employees), most agencies embody one of three cultures. but something is missing. In this culture, the agency owner will likely be controlling every detail, and not allowing the team any autonomy. The team is usually scared to make any decision without the approval of the agency owner. The agency owner has difficulty with delegating tasks, because of fear that the results won't be up to his/her standards.

The **"competition culture**" is a "compete" culture. Competition, goals, targets and deadlines are the focus. Reputation and success are most important to this culture. This organizational culture emphasizes winning and beating the competition. These agencies and their owners want to be the star in their field. It is about the recognition and goals. The owners of these agencies are usually commanding and demanding leaders. They push their team. This culture can achieve amazing results for the agency, but when this culture becomes a **"win at all cost"** culture, their agency will likely face compliance issues and team member turnover. The team members get burned out, over-worked, and then seek employment elsewhere.

The last culture is the "**people culture**." This culture is a collaborative culture. It is like a family where the leader is a mentor figure. Human development and long-term commitment to clients and the team are the key to this culture. With our small offices, it is easy to be like a family. There is loyalty between the team and the owner. There is teamwork and collaboration. But like a family, this culture can become dysfunctional. The owner becomes a parent-like figure and professional boundaries are crossed. The agency becomes more of a servicing agency than a production agency. The team begins to think "mom" or "dad" won't be mad if I don't hit these goals – they will understand.

Although your agency will have a dominant culture, I believe that to have a truly successful insurance agency, you must have a mix of these three cultures - the "**systems**," the "**people**", and the "**competition**" culture. You will have to adopt a " Wizard of Oz" mentality to manage these cultures, because your agency must have a mix of the brain, the heart, and the balls. (Yes, you are reading this correctly! I said it! Women leaders can have enormous lady balls!). There will be one dominant culture based on your personality as the owner of the agency, but there must be a combination of these three cultures for sustainable success. You have to give the "scarecrow a brain," the "tinman a heart," and the "lion some balls"!

I shared my story earlier. During my career, my agency has been all three of these cultures. It is about getting the mix right for you and your team. How many seminars or conferences have we all attended where a successful agency owner is instructing us on his/her system for creating the perfect agency? How often can you adopt their system and completely run your agency the same exact way? The answer is, "Never!" Many times, we can incorporate one or two nuggets from these presentations and incorporate them into our agency, but it is never a duplicate of their agency. Why?

Because you are not that other agency owner. You have your own strengths and challenges. You are not their clone. In addition, you have different team members with their own strengths and challenges.

No one will ever run their agency exactly like you, because they are not you. Just like you will not run your agency like the other agency owners, because you are not them. In the "**culture-based**" agency model, you take your strengths and create a culture that is based on you and your team. You work on the areas that will be a challenge for you, and you and your team continue the daily activities that will allow your agency to succeed. This culture and its success will be **"your unique mix!"**

In my agency, our dominant culture is the "**people culture.**" That is my personality and strength. This came easily in my agency, but I fell into the trap where I had no systems or accountability. I was the "friend" agent, not the respected leader. When I tried the "**systems culture**," it did not work. It was ineffective because I tried to be all systems, and that culture does not celebrate my strengths. To be truly successful in my agency, I had to integrate all three cultures. We have more systems in my agency than ever before. No, let me rephrase that – I actually have some systems! In addition, we have incorporated the competitive nature of the "**competition culture,**" so that we celebrate when we achieve our goals, and we hold each other accountable. A successful mix of these three cultures results in a tight-knit team that strives for goals - ethically and consistently.

• **Systems Culture Dominant:**

You, the agency owner and the leader of your team, sets the tone for the culture of the agency. You do so with the vision statement, but also with your personality. If you are a highly analytical person, your agency will always favor the "**systems culture.**" Your agency will have amazing systems, and you will have an in-depth training program for your team. In this culture, knowledge and systems are the key. Yet, this culture can get stuck in the details. This agent can overthink things and can't make the leap into action. The agency owner thinks and leads with his/her head.

To make this culture successful, you must add some "heart and balls." You have to take the strength of the "**competition culture**" and be fearless. Sometimes, you just have to jump in and take action. Your agency must develop that desire to strive and reach those goals, and you, the agent, cannot get bogged down in all the reports. Your team may be spending so much time documenting activities and placing them in the proper spread sheet, that they don't have time to sell.

You will also need to incorporate the **"people culture**" and show some "heart." An analytical agent doesn't need praise or words of affirmations, but your team does. This may be difficult for you, but you need to motivate your team by understanding **their** dreams and goals. You must show that you care, in order to receive full buy-in from them. In addition, your team members need some autonomy in order for their self-worth to grow. You could easily have the most amazing training system; but then, you have to relinquish some control, and let your team fly. Micro-managing will send your team into a reverse spin.

- **Competition Culture Dominant:**

If your agency is "**competition culture**" dominant, it usually means that the agency owner is a driven, type A personality. They push themselves to succeed and achieve goals. That expectation is passed on to their team members. In this culture, goals, production, and accolades are the key. The pitfalls for this culture often are compliance issues and team member burnout. The agency owner has some serious balls; and thus, can sometimes be a dick!

If you are constantly pushing your team members, they can become overwhelmed, overworked, and seek employment elsewhere. Or, more seriously, team members will take short cuts or find alternative ways to hit production numbers (i.e. the Wells Fargo scandal). Another danger of this culture are team members who become fixated on the next sale and become neglectful of current clients. Customer service is very likely to be an issue for this culture.

"**Competition culture**" is a direct path to success. The agency owner creates an environment where selling, selling, selling is rewarded. But to make this culture successful without compliance issues or employee turnover, it takes the heart of the **"people culture**" and the brains of the "**systems culture**." The agent/owner will have to slow down and teach systems correctly, and create and incorporate systems that will ensure compliant activity and sales. The agency owner will also have to find creative ways to motivate the team without fear. They will have to make goal achievement a part of the culture in a positive and motivating way.

- **People Culture Dominant:**

When the dominant culture is the "**people culture,**" the agency owner is usually all **"heart**." They care about their team members. They want their agency to have that "family vibe." They are invested in the lives and dreams of their team. The downside of this culture is that their "heart" will continually over-ride their "brains" and "balls." "**People culture**" agents often do not have defined systems. Everyone does their own thing and consistency is lacking. In addition, the agency owner can become too much of a "friend" to the team, resulting in the "best-friend" team members running over the owner. The agency owner starts to overlook employee issues or make excuses to retain unfit team members.

To make this culture successful, the agency owner needs to incorporate the "brains" and "balls" to build systems and accountability. He/she needs to put in standard operating procedures that all team members follow, and the team needs to be held accountable for these actions. This agency owner can think of fun and creative ways to motivate the team. They can usually get the buy-in from the team fairly easily based on their personality, but they need to work on being "respected by the team" versus "liked by the team."

Four steps to create your unique culture

There are four steps to creating
"your culture-mix of heart, brain, and balls!"

1) **Have an agency vision statement**: To create great culture, you have to start with a vision statement which gives the business a purpose. This is the guiding light that directs the business. This sets the tone of your culture. Depending on you, there will be a dominant-themed culture - (**People**, **Systems**, or **Competition)**, based on your vision statement.

2) **Team defines agency values**: The agency should have values, a set of guidelines for the behaviors and mindsets needed to achieve that vision. In creating these values, you incorporate the unique mix of your team. These will be the values that are important to them, so they will strive to live up to them.

3) **Incorporate all three cultures**: Make sure that all three cultures are reflected in your agency. There are components of each culture that must be incorporated into an agency to make it successful. We will explore these essential components soon.

4) **Culture X Disciplined execution = Business Excellence:** Finally, "**culture**" multiplied by

"**disciplined execution**" will create business excellence and agency success. Success will follow consistent daily practices – always!

In the following chapters, we will explore the inner workings of each step needed to create a dynamic culture in YOUR agency.

Step 1: Your Story

Create a vision statement for your agency

Every change begins with you. I shared how I tried to change my agency by putting in systems and expecting my employees to change. Real change occurred in my agency when I worked on myself. You are the only one who can control the actions that determine your life. You are the leader of your agency. You need to be the example for which your team strives. It doesn't mean that you are in the thick of it with your team making calls and answering billing questions. It means that you are providing the direction. You are the "lighthouse that directs the ships." It starts with you. No pressure, right?

In their book "The Business and Practice of Coaching," Lynn Grodzki and Wendy Allen said "*The day-to-day process of closely relating to your business will bring up everything – irrational thoughts, deeply held negatives beliefs, areas of your vulnerability – everything and anything unlike the cool, rational, businesslike attitude you would want to embody, for the purpose of your healing. . . Stop working so hard on your business, and let the business do its work on you.*" This process will be hard and can be somewhat painful when these irrational thoughts and negative beliefs hit us; but it is when we work through them, true growth occurs. Let's get started!

What is your story? You probably didn't grow up thinking you were going to be an insurance agent. What lead you to this profession? It's difficult to know the direction you want to pursue if you don't understand your purpose, your vision.

Let's start with an exercise. It is called a life journey exercise. In the space below, starting from your earliest memories, note all the significant events in your life. Note your birth, childhood, career highs and lows, relationships, and all the events that shaped you. (This exercise will not work well, unless you take the time to actually write down these events.)

Life Journey Exercise

____

Now, for each significant event, reflect on why these are significant? Were they positive or negative events? What emotion comes to you when you think of these events? How did they shape you to be the person you are today?

Then, think of the most influential person in your life. Who is that person and why did they make such an impact on you?

From this exercise, reflect on the values that are important to you. For example, the values that are important to me are loyalty, honesty, self-accountability, hard work, and compassion. What are the values that are most important to you? From these values, determine your personal vision statement. This is the statement that guides and directs your life. Mine is to be the best version of myself for my family, my friends, and my community.

This process may not come easily to you. It is a work in progress. It may change as time passes, but for now, put pen to paper. (This won't work unless it is written down.)

Your personal vision statement:

How did these values and your personal vision statement lead you to opening an agency? You could have started any business. Why was it your agency? What do you love about your insurance agency? Use these insights to determine your agency vision statement.

Your agency vision statement:

As mentioned before, this vision statement is the "lighthouse that guides your ship." Repetition and making it a daily part of your agency will set the culture of your agency in place. It should become part of the language of your team. Reading this vision statement should be done at every team meeting. It is the rally cry of your agency! Based on your vision statement, do you know what your dominant culture is? Recognize that you will have to incorporate elements of the other two cultures into your agency. Congratulations on taking the first step to create a winning, unique and dynamic team culture!

Step 2: The Team's Story

The values of the agency

Everything in the agency starts with you, the owner of the agency - your agency will grow or die based on the effectiveness of your team. If you have a great, talented team who are committed, your agency will thrive, but if you have a negative or ineffective team, your agency will flounder.

How do you get the commitment? People become more invested in something when it is their idea. They gain commitment when it is "their words." You as the leader gave them the direction with your vision statement. Now, your team will come up with the values together. Values are the set of beliefs that your team will honor, hold dear and follow. The Harvard Review Journal stated that values are, *"a set of guidelines on the behaviors and mindsets needed to achieve that vision."* These values are the guidelines that will dictate the actions and attitude of the team.

How to come up with the values? Really, just ask! Ask your team what values they want to see reflected in the agency. Ask them what values come to mind when they read the vision statement. This can be done in a team meeting. There are no wrong answers. Write down everything they say. There is no correct number of values. You may have 50 written on the board. There may be some similar ones like trustworthy or honesty. Get clarification from your team. Ask them what they meant by those words. Then ask them if the two words are similar in meaning. If so, you then vote on the word that most resonates with the team. When you do this exercise, most teams come up with 10-15 values.

My agency's vision is to "bee" a difference in the lives of the people on our team, our agency, and our community. How can we actually "bee" a difference? Our values are "bee" committed, "bee" kind, "bee" grateful, "bee" a person of integrity, "bee" accountable, "bee" passionate, "bee" knowledgeable, "bee" inspiring and "bee" fearless. I know, cheesy! We all came up with them together and review them annually, so that we can revise them each year if needed. We commit to upholding these values in our agency.

Because your team came up with their values, you can ask them to commit to them. Now you have buy-in. We also rate ourselves on each value. On a scale of 1-10, how would you rate yourself on each value? If you are going to commit to these values, you need to be clear on what values might be a breeze for you or a struggle. We share our insights with the group. For example, I have difficulty with "bee accountable," and "bee inspiring" is easier for me. I can definitely be flaky, but I have agreed to these values and will work on this. Also, I can celebrate my strengths. By "beeing" inspiring, I can come up with fun and creative ideas for the agency. Since we ourselves are acknowledging our challenges, this also allows everyone on the team to hold up a mirror for each other when we are not living up to the values.

Now everything in the agency comes back to the vision and the values. When we have an issue in our office, we ask the team member, "Are you living up to the value of being accountable?" It is just putting up a mirror for the team. If you have the right team, you won't have to discipline. You will just have to remind them of the values. With the right team, they will own up to their mistakes or shortcomings. The larger issue is, will **You**, as the agency owner, look into the same mirror and honor the true reflection. I'm not saying that this is easy!

Step 3: Incorporate All Three Cultures

Based on the personality of the agent and their team, there will be a dominant culture in your agency. To ensure the greatest success for your agency, all three, **Systems**, **People**, and **Competition** cultures must be reflected. In this chapter, we will discuss the three essential components of these cultures.

• **Three Essential Components of the Systems culture:**

1) Systems

The strength of the systems culture is the, duh, systems! Surprise! Systems are important in an insurance agency, because it creates consistency. Everyone in the agency is quoting the same way, explaining coverages the same way, and agency building activities are consistently being done daily.

In every agency, there should be a written system for everything. There are agency "building" and agency "maintaining" activities. Agency "building activities" are those that generate and produce agency growth and income. Examples of agency building activities are quoting, marketing, and pivoting. We call these money-making activities in our agency. Agency "maintaining activities" are those that maintain the current book of business. Examples of agency "maintaining activities" are calling on late payments, processing claims, and scanning forms.

Whether it is an agency "building" or agency "maintaining" activity, there should be a clearly written system (SOP, a standard operating procedure) for each of these activities. Probably, one of the most important systems is the system for hiring and training amazing team members.

Many agency owners say that they have systems in their head, but it is not written down. It needs to be written down as a reference guide to everyone on the team. It may be a system in your head, but is it the same system in the minds of your team member? I know that I am always forgetting things, and I have to go back to my notes for clarification. As I am writing this book, I can recall instances when I write a word, and I am 90% sure I spelled it correctly, but it just doesn't look right? So, what do I do? I use spell check just to confirm that I spelled it correctly. That is what the written systems will be. They will be a reference - your spell check. You might have the memory of an elephant, but your team members might struggle. Systems are about consistency, and if the team forgets the systems, they can reference your written "**systems manual.**"

You can create your own systems or borrow systems from other agency owners. There are plenty of agents out there that would be happy to share their systems, but most importantly, make sure that they work for you and your team. Remember, your agency is unique and what works for one agency may not work for another agency. If it's not working for you, don't be afraid to let go.

2) Know your Numbers

The second essential component from the "**systems culture"** is knowing your numbers. Marcus Lemonis said, "*If you don't know your numbers, you don't know your business.*" There are many agency owners that do not run their agency as a business. I have been guilty of this in the past. Many of us were not entrepreneurs before we opened our agency. Truthfully, many of us are not "numbers" people, but how can you effectively run a business if you don't know your numbers?

So, what are the important numbers?

Gross Revenue and Expenses:

First, in any business, what is your gross revenue and what are your expenses? In terms of your gross revenue, what is your compensation on each insurance product? Many agency owners do not have a clear understanding of how they are compensated. Truthfully, it is complicated. You may have multiple carriers who have different compensation plans. Your agency may have different compensations for the same product (for example, you may be compensated more for personally produced business versus website-initiated business.) Frankly, as an agency owner, you will probably never fully understand every detail of your compensation, but you must have a clear understanding of it in order to strategize a plan to achieve maximum compensation.

If you want to increase your gross revenue for the year, what are the numbers needed to achieve that – i.e. how many auto policies, fire policies, etc ? There is new business compensation and there are lapses and cancellations. Taking into account the cancellations/lapses, how much would you have to grow in order to hit your goal? In our industry, we have units and premium.

We can grow by units and decrease in premium or we can increase by premium and decrease in units. How so? If your company has a rate increase, you will see an increase in your overall premium, but there may be more cancellations of policies. This would result in fewer units (fewer policies), or vice versa. Your company can have a rate decrease. Therefore, your overall book would see a premium decrease, but your agency may be writing more units, and you will grow in units (policies). During this time of rate decreases, do you invest in your business (take home less money) to grow the maximum number of units, so that when rates increase, you will receive a higher increase? You must understand your numbers to make this decision.

In addition, what are your expenses? Are there ways to reduce your expenses? The biggest expense for insurance agencies is payroll. Are your team members paying for themselves? Remember, there are other costs associated with employees such as health insurance, 401K, and other benefits. In addition, payroll taxes and worker's comp also factor into the cost of an employee. What production is required of that team member in order for you to get your (ROI) return on investment?

What are your other expenses, and are you getting the best deal on each of them? Every expense should be reviewed on an annual basis when you do your business planning and budgeting. If you know that your rent will increase 3% next year, will your revenue generate enough to cover that increase or will you have to cut some other expenses in your budget.

Many agency owners complete a simple business plan with production numbers, and a goal for how much they want to produce next year. Unfortunately, many do not complete a business plan for their budget. What will be their expenses and projected income next year? Will there be rate increases or decreases that will affect gross income? A budget and a projected profit and loss should be part of your business plan every year.

If your personality naturally gravitates toward the "**systems culture,**" you may go down a rabbit hole with these numbers and try to calculate numbers exactly. Be aware of your natural tendencies and that you may be over-analyzing. On the opposite end, if your personality naturally gravitates towards "**competition**" or "**people culture**," these numbers might be overwhelming. Just do your best and don't forget you can always ask for help. Ask your CPA. Does your company have a regional manager that can help you with these numbers? In addition, having a better understanding of these numbers (not perfectly - just better) is still 1000% better than not understanding your numbers at all.

Numbers for money-making activities

Now that you have an understanding of your gross compensation and how you are paid for the different policies/carriers, what are your goals for the year? Do you want to maintain or do you want to grow your book of business? If you are in growth mode, how much do you want to grow?

We own a business, and at the end of the day, we want to make money. If you are at a point in your career where you are happy with your net profit, then you are in "agency maintenance." If this is the case, you need to first review your expenses for next year. What will be the increases in your annual expenses for rent, payroll, utilities? Then, on average how many policies do you lose annually due to cancellations or lapses? What is the gross compensation on those policies?

Let's say that your total expenses this year were $150,000. Taking into account inflation and rent increase, your expenses will increase by 3% next year, approximately $4500. Your agency loses approximately 200 policies a year due to cancellations and lapses, which equates to a $12,000 loss annually ($600 annual premium multiplied by 200 times 10% commission). I made up these numbers for the example, but your company or carrier will have reports that can calculate this for you.

Using these numbers, if your agency does not generate any new business, it will lose $16,500 next year ($4,500+$12,000). If you wish to keep your income at the same level as the prior year, you will have to generate $16,500 in new business to offset your losses. How?

Let's say that $600 is your average premium and your commission is 10%. That means you get paid $60 a year per policy. If you need to generate $16,500 in income, divide $16,500 by $60. That comes to 275. That means you will have to produce 275 policies that year or 23 policies a month.

Now comes your money-making activities numbers. If your agency needs to produce 23 policies per month, then how many quotes will you have to do? What is your agency conversion ratio? Again, your company and/or carrier will have reports that will assist you with this. Let's say that your conversion ratio is 25%. This means that you will need to do four quotes to write one policy. Therefore, to produce 23 policies, you will have to complete 92 quotes per month. If your conversion ratio is 10% (1 policy per 10 quotes), then you must complete 230 quotes.

Let's break this down a little further. Let's say your agency rocks and has a 25% conversion ratio. You have to do 92 quotes per month. There are an average of 20 work days per month. That means you have to complete (92 divided by 20) 4.6 or 5 quotes per day. How do you get new quotes? In my agency, we get quotes through walk-ins (quotes that organically enter our agency), marketing calls (we call on old quotes), pivots (pivoting to another line of insurance with an existing customer), and referrals (from existing customers or circles of influence).

If you have not been tracking your marketing sources, you will not have accurate numbers. For now, take an educated guess - but in the future, start tracking. I will cover tracking in the next section. The educated guess will just give you a starting point.

On a day-to-day basis, we can't really control walk-in quotes. This is controlled by marketing and social media. For the point of this exercises, let's say on average you get one walk in quote per day. In my agency, I don't count the walk-ins. They are the bonus. They are not determined by our day-to-day activities, so we do not account for them when we are planning our money-making activities.

That means, your agency will need to complete five quotes through marketing calls, pivoting, and asking for referrals. On average, I believe that it takes 10 marketing calls to get one quote. Therefore, if you are trying to get four quotes, your agency needs to make 40 calls a day. For pivoting, let's say that three (3) pivots will net you one (1) quote. And finally, five (5) referral asks will net one (1) quote. Referrals are almost a double ask. You have to convince the customer to give you the names of friends and family. Then you have to persuade the friend/family to allow you to give them a quote.

Now what is the right mix for your agency? If you are trying for five (5) quotes, let's say that you are able to obtain three (3) from marketing calls, one (1) from a pivot, and one (1) from referrals. That converts to your agency needing to make 30 calls, three (3) pivots, and five (5) referral asks a day. These are your money-making activities.

Next how do you split them up amongst your team members, and how do you hold them accountable? We will discuss these in the next sections. In summary, to be successful, you need a clear understanding of your numbers, your gross profit, expenses, and money-making activities.

Now if you are in a growth mode in your agency, how much do you want to grow? Let's use the example above for your agency. To maintain, you need to write $16,500 in premium that year. Let's say you want to make an additional $20,000. That means you need to write at least $36,500 in premium. Now break down your numbers the same way.

Let's say that $600 is your average premium and your commission is 10%. That means you get paid $60 a year per policy. If you need to generate $36,500 in income, divide $36,500 by $60. That comes to 608. That means you will have to produce 608 policies that year, or 51 policies a month.

Now comes your money-making activities numbers. If your agency needs to produce 51 policies per month, then how many quotes will you have to complete? What is your agency conversion ratio? Again, your company and/or carrier will have reports that will assist you with this. Let's say that your conversion ratio is 25%. That means that you will need to complete four quotes to write one policy. So, to produce 51 policies, you will have to complete 204 quotes per month. How many quotes is that per working day? Now break down your money-making activities the same way – how many marketing calls, pivots and referrals will need to be completed each day?

Understanding these numbers outlines for your agency the daily activities that will ensure success. Just like eating right and exercising each day will benefit your physical health, completing these money-making activities will benefit your agency production

3) Tracking :

Now that you have your systems in place and understand your numbers, you must have a system for tracking these numbers. Why? Tracking allows you and your agency to see your progress and make corrections along the way. In addition, tracking keeps the goals fresh and relevant on a consistent basis.

Ugghhhh – I am constantly dieting and exercising. I used to get really mad, because I felt that I was eating right, but I wasn't seeing the result on the scale. When I started tracking my diet (logging in my food), I started noticing how often I cheat. I also noticed that some of the foods I was eating had a higher calorie count than I thought. Just like this example, tracking allows valuable insight into your agency.

What things should I track? I track revenue and expenses. I use " Quickbooks" for my book keeping, but I am also old-school and use an Excel spreadsheet to track my agency premiums on a monthly basis. I also track monthly production. I track my whole team and individual team member productions. There are some great programs out there that will help you with this. I have tried some of them, but I keep coming back to my Excel spreadsheets. They work for me. Any program that works for you, is a good program. Just use one!

In my agency, we also track the money-making activities. Money-making activities are those activities that generate sales. Based on our growth numbers, we have calculated our money-making activities. We track pivots, calls, and referrals. Tracking these activities on a daily basis encourages good daily habits. I create binders for each team member every month. I print these out in my office and take them to Office Depot to be coil bound. These binders allow my team to plan their day, and to track their money-making activities. An example of these pages is on the next page. At the end of the day, my team enters their numbers on an Excel spreadsheet (like I said, I love them), and I review these numbers with my team on a weekly basis.

Today's Plan

Date:

	My Awesome Plan for the Day!
8:30 AM	
9:00 AM	
9:30 AM	
10:00 AM	
10:30 AM	
11:00 AM	
11:30 AM	
12:00 PM	
12:30 PM	
1:00 PM	
1:30 PM	
2:00 PM	
2:30 PM	
3:00 PM	
3:30 PM	
4:00 PM	
4:30 PM	
5:00 PM	

Main Goal for Today? ______________________________

Today's Top Activities To Achieve Goal:

Pivots (3 pivots) :

Referral Asks (3):

Review Asks (3):

Appointment Asks (2):

Appointments Conducted (1) :

Marketing Calls (20 Marketing Calls):

• Three Essential Components of the Competition Culture:

1) Clearly defined roles, goals, and expectations:

The main focus of the "**competition culture**" is goals; therefore, the goals must be clear to everyone. The goals of the agency should be known by the whole team. The goals can't be nebulous like, "let's have a successful year." Don't laugh! – that has been my single goal in the past. From the "numbers" discussion, I repeat, **"know your numbers**!" What are the goals of the agency? And what are the goals and expectations of each team member?

What exactly is the job description for each? What is their role? If they have been hired for sales, what is their production goal? What do you expect them to achieve each month? What is the bare minimum production you expect, and if they are not achieving that, what are the consequences? If they are hired for service, what exact functions fall into this category? What is the metric by which you will evaluate their performance; and if they don't hit that metric, what are the consequences? We will discuss accountability more in performance reviews.

As an agency owner, you may believe that you are extremely clear with your expectations. You may believe that the team clearly understands his/her role. There have been times that I have been shocked when a team member did not clearly understand the role. Sometimes more repetition is needed. That is why these expectations are discussed in the weekly team meetings and in their monthly performance reviews. You should repeat these goals so many times that it is engraved in their minds. In my agency, we have organizational charts that clearly explain their duties and outline the production expectations for each team member.

This step is critical because it has been proven that when a goal is displayed visually, and when a goal is repeated constantly, the chances that the goal will be achieved are greatly increased. If you fail to display the goals and to repeat them frequently, you cannot blame your staff – the failure is yours alone. They concluded, and rightfully so, that you are no longer interested in that goal – that it wasn't that important.

2) Time Management: *Prioritize money making activities*

In the numbers section, we discussed the money-making activities. Although our culture is clearly a **"people culture,"** at the end of the day, we are a business. Businesses have to make money to stay in business. Every year, businesses have to make more money to give their employees raises and pay the rising costs of utilities, rent, and supplies. Therefore, no matter how much you care about your clients and strive to give them the best customer service, your business has to make money. If you don't, you will no longer have a business.

That means, sales have to be priority over customer services. All the **"people culture"** agents are just cringing. I know! As a "**people culture**" agency, we absolutely care about our clients and go above and beyond for them, but we understand that our time is limited. We only have eight hours a day, and in those eight hours, our money-making activities (sales activities) must come first.

Don't get me wrong. We are there to assist our clients especially when there is a claim, but there are some service items that can be streamlined for efficiency or maybe just aren't necessary functions. My office used to call clients at least three times regarding late payments and forms. We now give our customers three touches (text, email, and call), since they already receive mail directly from the insurer. This was such a difficult change for my team. We didn't want our customers to have a lapse in their insurance, so we were constantly reminding them. Yet this was so time consuming. If we were going to ensure that money- making activities were primary, something had to be dropped.

I am not advising you to do the same for your office. Again, you need to run your office the way it works for you, but you must make sales a priority. If you are "crushing it" with your production and your sales activity and still have time for multiple follow-ups, go for it! I have just found that in my agency, there is only so much time; and when we incorporate something new, many times we need to drop something else.

Agencies that are "**competition culture"** do this naturally. Many times, their agencies have a call center type environment. They always make sales and money-making activities a priority, and by so doing, their environment becomes like a call center. This is not my agency. I am a "**people culture"** agency; therefore, we love customer service, but we understand that we need to make sales the number one priority. Make sure that sales are a priority and run your office accordingly.

3) Performance Reviews:

You have given your team the goals and numbers. You have also made their roles and expectations extremely clear to them. Although it is up to them to execute, they may still need more help with training and accounting. For a task to be completed, one must have the willingness to do the task and the capacity to perform it. Your team member may want to get it done, but they may not have the capacity. You may have given them the numbers, and made your expectations clear to them, but if they do not have the training, the task will not be completed.

Therefore, your agency needs to implement a good training program. In terms of systems, I believe that this is where most agencies struggle. Then, the agency owner must conduct performance reviews that evaluate their performance and provide some additional training or mentorship. In my agency, we have a set training program for new team members. For new team members, we have a 30 day, 60 day, and 90 day performance review. For more seasoned team members, we also have a monthly performance review and an annual performance review. Our numbers are broken down monthly. Some agencies follow the twelve-week year. Again, make this work for the system you implement in your office. Since our numbers are monthly, the team member's goals and expectations are evaluated on a monthly basis. I expect them to produce a certain number of applications and premium monthly. If these expectations are not met, we discuss what were the obstacles. If they need additional training, I provide that training. If it is fear or self-sabotaging behavior, we discuss techniques to overcome this.

As a "**people culture**" agency, I will invest a little more time in team members to get them to achieve these goals. "**Competition**" agencies generally move faster to terminate an employee who is not meeting goals. This is more difficult for me. Yet, I know that I had to incorporate more of the "**competition culture**." That is why in my agency, I have to see activity and improvement. If I can see that a team member has the capacity (the intelligence), and the willingness to do the work, and they are performing the money- making activities, I am willing to work a little longer with them as long as they are showing improvement. I also need to be honest in my assessment of them. I have terminated team members that did not have the mental capability to complete the job no matter how much they tried. I have also terminated team members because I wanted them to succeed more than they did.

As a "**people culture**" agency, I am willing to invest a little more time in my team members, but my boundaries are clear. The performance reviews provide an opportunity to have a honest discussion with my team members. The good ones will use these reviews to find areas of improvement. The bad ones will use these to determine that working in your agency is not a good fit.

• Three Essential Components of the People culture:

1) Leadership, understanding team dynamics and communication:

As stated in the earlier chapter, true change starts with you as the owner of the agency. As the leader, you have taken the first step. You created a vision statement that is the direction and guiding force of your agency. Now you must live the values and the vision of your agency. You can't lead others until you become the leader of your own behavior, and you can't run an agency by yourself. Therefore, there is no way to avoid leadership responsibilities - you must lead your team!

Leadership is such an extensive word. There are thousands of books on leadership. Leadership can be defined in so many ways, but true leadership starts with you. Owning a business brings out the best and the worst in us. It shows us our strengths, but it also shows us our challenges. Any business will face major hurdles until we work on ourselves. My strengths are that I am fun, kind, and creative; but placing boundaries, and follow-through are my challenges, and I must own that.

Before I worked on myself and the culture of my agency, my strengths and challenges were reflected in my agency. I am fun and kind, so my employees generally liked me, but I had difficulty placing boundaries, so I was extremely lax with my employees. I also had a hard time with follow through. I would come back from a meeting or seminar and implement a new system for my office. We would do it for about three weeks and then, it would stop. Does that sound familiar? My agency definitely incorporated the strengths of the "**people culture**," but there was very little evidence of the "**systems"** or **"competition culture."** The "**people culture"** is easy for me based on my personality; therefore, I knew that I would have to work on the elements of the other cultures.

Since one of our values is being accountable, I knew that I too had to be really accountable. I couldn't put a mirror to my team about our values without doing the same for myself. Your team does not expect you to be perfect. They expect you to try your hardest. I don't expect my team to be perfect. Just try their hardest. Leadership starts with vulnerability. Vulnerability in leadership is not weakness - it is strength.

When we were putting the <u>values</u> in place, I told my team that I was going to have a hard time with accountability. Follow-through is tough for me. I was vulnerable and honest, but I said that I would do my best to live up to those values. They also had my full permission to hold up the mirror for me. Then I honored my commitment. This does not mean that I am perfect. It means I do my best. We business owners have our strengths and challenges, and each team member will have their unique mix of strength and challenges, as well. There are several amazing personality and strength assessments out there. If you are willing to help your team members discover their strengths and challenge; and then shine the light on their strengths, and mentor them while they work on their challenges, they will reward you with loyalty, creativity and hard work.

An effective leader also must have good communication skills. Truthfully, effective communication is the key to almost everything. Effective communication affects our personal lives, how we relate to our family and friends. It also affects work. Effective communication is the foundation of a strong "**people culture.**" As a leader, how do you communicate with your team?

True leadership occurs when we inspire people. It does not happen when we lead with fear. As an employer or leader, many agency owners lead their team through fear. (If you don't perform or produce, you are fired.) It's that threat of termination that keeps the team performing, but usually, the environment is a toxic one. Employees are generally unhappy or they start doing unethical things to make numbers (remember the Wells Fargo scandal – Beware!)

Some agency owners are the opposite and are too lax. They want their employees to like them and want to be their friend. This also creates a negative culture. It's a culture of laziness and complacency. In this situation, it's usually the agent that is extremely unhappy and checked-out of their business. In the same way as the fear culture, your team is not inspired. They are not unhappy, but they don't find fulfillment in their work. This was the culture of my office. I was the lax leader that didn't set the boundaries for my team members.

So how do we inspire our team? As leaders of our agency, we need to be firm but compassionate. The most effective way is to communicate effectively. Together, we crafted a "vision statement" and "values statement" for our agency. This is the "why" behind all our actions, and it becomes part of the language of our agency. For example, in our agency, we talk about our vision and values statement during the first interview. We ask all candidates if this is something they can commit to. If not, this is not the agency for them. We are all human; therefore imperfect, but we strive to live up to the values. When this concept is firmly in place, there generally won't be any need for discipline. We simply have to ask team members to live up to the values and remind them when they fall short.

I am not saying that all employees will be perfect, but you will know which ones fit the culture or which ones don't. You will know when it is time to cut bait. It won't be as hard to let someone go, because they knew that they were not living up to the values they came up with and agreed to. This is the most effective communication tool, because we established clarity and buy-in. As leaders, we don't have to threaten or be their friend. All we have to do is ask them to live up to their commitments. We also have to incorporate parts of the "**competition culture**" and have the "balls" to fire team members who do not fit our culture.

As stated earlier, communication is clarity. In all my communication, I also try and explain the reasons for my requests or actions. It's not that we have to justify our actions. It's so they understand the importance of them.

I do this all the time with my children. For example, "why is it important for them to get a good grade? So, they can go to a good college. Why is it important to go to a good college? It gives them opportunities and time to decide on a career path. Why is it important to have a career? So, we can have money for our family. Why is that important? So, we can have a happy life." In other words, as owners we need to take as much time to think out how we are communicating with our team as we do with our family. It's that important!

Obviously, I don't do this exact type of questioning with my team, but I make sure that they understand the **reason** for my requests. For example, when I ask them to make marketing calls, they understand that so many marketing calls equate to quotes. So many quotes turn into sales. So many sales add to the overall gross revenue of the agency, which is then returned to them in the form of bonuses, raises, etc.

I believe that leadership starts with the owner of the agency. Through your personal growth by fostering your strengths and working on your challenges, you start on the road to creating an amazing business. Leadership is also effective communication, and finally, leadership is mentorship!

To be a mentor is to provide guidance to your team. When you help your team achieve their goals, there is no better way to achieve team member engagement. Inspirational leadership comes from mentorship. This mentorship comes from helping your team achieve their dreams and goals. It can be hiring a student who works for you while they are pursuing a degree. It can be mentoring a team member to open their own insurance agency. It can be teaching them financial skills, coaching them on work and personal goals, or working on communication skills.

Work affects our personal lives, and our personal lives affects our work. Just like you the leader, when a team member works on their personal growth, their production at work will increase. When we can mentor our team through their personal growth, the agency will reap the rewards. Mentoring your team to live up to the values they stated, also helps create and maintain the culture of your agency.

2) Team personal development, goals, and dreams:

One of the most important roles we have as agency owners is the role of mentor. We need to be a mentor for our team members. If we have the right people in place, they will work diligently for our agencies. If those team members are not achieving their full potential, it not only hurts them, but it hurts us and our agencies.

First, it is our role to train them properly. This was covered in the "**systems**" portion. This would include training them on the products, sales techniques, and systems. In my agency, the training does not stop with product knowledge and sales techniques. We also train for personal development. In my agency, personal development means communication skills, health, meditation, overcoming fears and self-limiting beliefs, understanding personal finance and investments and even relationships.

There are millions of books written on personal development. Pick one and read it together at the office. We read one chapter at a time and discuss it at our team meeting. Personal life affects work, and work affects personal life. It is almost impossible to separate the two.

I have noticed that when I am doing better with my diet and exercise, it seems like all aspects of my life are operating more smoothly. My agency becomes amazing! I joke that my agency gross revenue is inversely linked to my body weight. As my weight goes down, my agency produces more. I don't know why, but it just does. Personal affects work. Many times, our team members struggle because of their personal lives. If we can give them the tools to change their personal lives for the better, it will carry over into their work.

In addition, helping our team with their personal development means assisting them with reaching their dreams and their goals. I remember when my office manager bought her first home. When we started our **agency culture model**, she made a personal goal of reducing debt. Then, the following year when she achieved that goal, she made another one to save money for a house. I recall the pride she felt when she achieved this goal. I think we both teared up. My eyes still tear up when I think of how proud I am of her accomplishment. There is no better way to foster commitment and loyalty than when you help a team member achieve their goal. You show them you care. Now her goal is a new, bigger house!

Sometimes mentoring a team member means giving them the tools they need to pursue their dreams outside of your agency. When my former team member, Jason Paszek, left my agency to open his own, I was proud and sad. I was proud of his accomplishment, but I just lost an amazing team member. As a leader, you hope that your great team member never leaves you, but you cannot stifle their personal growth. You will only end up with an unhappy disgruntled team member. You can give incentives to entice them to stay, but at the end of the day, they will make the decision that is best for them, because you gave them the tools to achieve their goals. In addition, if you are mentoring your team, your agency will continue to flourish even when a strong team member leaves, because every team member is amazing!

3) Fun:

Our field of insurance involves a lot of customer service. Unfortunately, in the insurance industry, the customer service aspect can be hard on our team members – they get "beat-up" a lot. They deal with customers in some of the worst situations of their lives. So, there are times that our customers are not particularly kind to our team members. In addition, insurance is not necessarily a fun topic for the public. Therefore, to keep team members engaged, we have to make agency fun. How do we do that?

First, as agency owners, we need to applaud every "win," even the small ones. We need to give praise and appreciation for our team members. Sometimes, especially if our personalities favor the "**competition"** or "**systems"** culture, agency owners tend to say, "It's their job, why do I need to praise or thank them? I pay them!"

Early in my marriage, my husband and I were having arguments over household chores. I did not feel that he was doing his fair share of the daily chores. (A typical wife's battle cry!) He would do the dishes; but I was still upset, because I felt that I did much more. (of course!) No matter how many dishes he did, I was still nagging. One day, I realized that maybe I should try a different approach. He did the dishes, and I gave him praise. In fact, you would have thought he had cured cancer with how much praise he received! I really just wanted to say, "that's the least you could do!" But, instead, I showered him with praise. Guess what happened? He continued to do the dishes and started taking on more household chores. Boy, lesson learned!

In the same manner, when team members receive praise and feel appreciated, they will want to do more. It might start off small like doing their marketing calls, but once the praise starts rolling in, your team will want to do more. We are social animals. We love compliments and helping our team. In my agency, when one of our team members has a "win," we all stop and jointly give them praise. Plus, compliments are just fun! One **"systems culture"** agent joked that he is going to schedule compliments on his calendar. I know he was joking, but whatever works! If you need to schedule a compliment, do it!

A second way to incorporate some fun into your agency is to arrange activities outside of the agency - some team building activities. Before Covid, our office tried to do something each quarter. It ended up being more like every six months. We have done a cancer 5k run; we have volunteered at a local food bank; we have had pool parties; we have done escape rooms; we have had potlucks in the office, and we have also just gone to local "happy hours." We also do one big Fall planning event. Last year, I took my team on a hot air balloon ride; and this year, we drove racecars on the Las Vegas Speedway.

A third way to bring more fun into your agency is to introduce playful competitions and promotions. Be creative! Not all promotions need to be monetary. One quarter, we had a promotion for any life or health policies sold. If you sold a policy, you got to draw a prize. The prices were different denominations of cash ($5, $10, $20, or $50), but there were also random "dollar store" items.

We have also challenged other agencies to friendly competitions for lunch. This year the theme for my agency is "On the Fast Track." We went to the Las Vegas Speedway and raced Ferraris. Our tracking board now has race cars with our individual pictures. If you are not creative, use the strengths of your team members. I bet one of your team members is "**people culture**" oriented. This team member can help you to come up with lots of creative ideas.

You just have to incorporate fun into your agency! And, amazingly, you are going to have fun too!

Two components that incorporate all three cultures:

1)Weekly Team meetings

If you are going to only incorporate one thing from this book into your agency, I recommend that it is the weekly team meeting. The weekly team meeting should be done consistently on a weekly basis at a set time with an "agenda." Many agents say that setting a weekly meeting at the same time is too difficult – it can't be done. But, if it's not on the calendar consistently, it becomes too easy to skip it when we get busy. The weekly team meeting incorporates all three cultures, the **"systems," "people," and "competition;"** therefore, if you were only going to do one thing, this would give you the most bang. Sometimes setting the meeting an hour or half hour before opening will work.

I will show you the agenda for our team meeting, but like everything in this book, make it work for you and your team. As long as you are doing weekly team meetings with an agenda, you are miles ahead of many agencies.

1) **Vision and Values Statements (People)**– We read this aloud at the start of each meeting. This is a weekly reminder of our agency "vision" and the "values" we all committed to.

2) **Opening word (People)** – Just an opening word about how we are feeling that morning. This is a check in for each team member. If they say something like frazzled, we know that they are having a rough morning.

3) **Ice-breaker (People)** – This can be a game or just an icebreaker question. It's a way to have fun and get to know each other better.

4) **Numbers (Competition)** – We discuss our production numbers as a team and individually. We determine our progress towards our goals. We also discuss individual money-making activities for each team member. We are holding each other accountable. (the mirror)

5) **Headlines (Systems) -**
   a) Attendance - Is anyone off next week?
   b) Compliance/Issues – This started off as a way of tracking whether team members were following our procedures, but now it has become a way to discuss any issues from the previous week.
   c) Any other headlines - Do we have any training sessions lined up? Any study groups next week? Company announcements or promotions?

This is where I list everything I wanted to discuss with my team during the week. Previously, I was constantly interrupting my team with non-urgent matters like training reminders. This can wait until the team meeting.

6) **Presentations/Training (Systems**) - my team takes turns doing a 5 to 10 minute presentation on a topic of their choice. It could be about life sales or time management. If I have something, I will present, but we all take turns.

7) **Personal Development (People)** - We pick a book and read a chapter per week. We discuss the major takeaways from the book. This is about personal development for every person on the team. The books can be about insurance or a completely different topic as long as it is a personal development book. We had a great time reading about the love languages!

8) **Accountability (Competition) -** During this section my team commits to one personal and one professional goal for the week.

9) **Closing word (People) -** This is a mindset exercise. Every meeting ends with a positive word from each participant.

As you can see, a set agenda team meeting incorporates parts of each culture. The "**people culture"** provides personal development. Goals and accountability are refined by the "**competition culture**" and the "**systems culture**" directs us to the training schedule. That is why if you are going to do only **<u>one</u>** thing recommended by this book, let it be a well-run weekly team meeting.

2) Annual Strategy/Fall Planning Meeting

If you were planning to do **<u>two</u>** things from this book, the next thing I would recommend is the "annual strategy/fall planning" meeting. The annual strategy meeting is important for your agency, because it gives your team some time to reflect on the successes and the challenges of the year. This allows them the opportunity to continue the behaviors that created success and to redirect or change things to remedy the challenges. This is the planning and goal setting needed in order to ensure that the next year is just as amazing as the last!

I will show you the agenda for our fall planning meeting, but again, like everything in this book, make it work for you and your team. As long as you are doing fall planning with an agenda, you are ahead of the game. This is a four-hour long meeting. I usually schedule this on a Saturday from 10:00 am. to 2:00 pm. when we are closed. To make it less formal, I do it at my home, and I cater lunch for the team.

This is the agenda:

a) **Year in review (Competition**) - We discuss the successes and challenges of the agency as a whole this year. We also share our individual successes and challenges. We then outline what we could have done better individually, me as a leader, and as an agency.

b) **Values and recommitment to the values (People)** - Every year, we reassess our values. Some we keep, some we delete, and we add new ones. We do this every year, because we may have some new team members. In addition, we should have progressed this past year and other values might have gained in priority. After we agree on our values, we once again re-evaluate ourselves based on these values. Are there values that are easy for us? Are there values that will be more difficult? Then we all recommit to living these values day in and day out in our agency.

c) **Goals for next year (Competition) and (Systems)** - What are our goals for next year as an agency? As the agency leader, I set these numbers using guidelines set forth by my parent company. I also set these based on projected profit goals. I know the monetary number I want to increase by every year, then I work backwards like I explained during the "numbers" discussion in the earlier chapter. These numbers are presented to the team and discussed.

I also break down these numbers for each team member. If our agency goal is to write 200 policies a month and we have four team members, each team member should write 50 policies. I explain exactly how I came up with these numbers. I feel that my team should make more money every year, but the numbers have to support that. This is the gross revenue increase we need to generate in order to give raises. If the team has questions or suggestions, we might tweak these numbers.

There have been years when we decreased our production numbers, and there have been years when the team believed we could do better than the numbers I presented! Here is the bottom line for my team - they clearly understand that if we do not increase our gross profit, they will not make more money. These are the numbers that we need to generate for them to increase their income.

d) **Personal commitments (Systems, Competition, and People**) - We then come up with one personal and one work goal for ourselves. What do we want to accomplish for ourselves personally and professionally next year? Many times, the goals are tied to one another. For example, I want to buy a home next year, which means I need to make an additional $10,000. Like I stated previously, you can't separate work from personal and personal from work. So, a personal goal would be to buy a home, and the work goal would be to increase income by $10,000. We then "smartize" these goals. SMART stands for specific, measurable, attainable, realistic, and trackable. What is the specific goal? (To save for the house.) Is it measurable? (I need to save $10,000 for the down payment). Is it attainable? (These are the production goals I will need to achieve in order to make $10,000 more this year). Is it realistic? Can you make that production goal? Do you have the capacity and the desire to make it happen? Is it trackable, and do you have a tracking system in place?

By doing this, you as the agency owner are helping your team members achieve their goals and dreams, as well as your own. Everyone on the team profits – It's a win/win!

e) **Training (Systems) -** We have done sales training. We have also done personal development training. One year the team learned how agency gets paid. This year, I may bring in a speaker for our training.

f) **Lunch, Team building exercise, and some fun (People) -** We take a 30 minute lunch break and just spend some time together. This allows us to just enjoy each other's company as a group. I personally incorporate games into the whole day. There is a prize at the end of the day for the winner. This keeps team members engaged and having fun.

   We also do a team building exercise. One year, we did a paint party. Now, we do the team building activity the next day (Sunday). We have done hot air balloon riding, and this year we drove exotic vehicles on the racetrack. It's important to keep things fresh and fun for your team.

As stated earlier, the weekly team meeting and the fall planning agenda both incorporate all three cultures. If you are only planning to do **two** things from this book, these will help your agency the most. The strategy/ fall planning meeting sets the goals for the coming year for your agency. The weekly team meeting tracks the progress of these goals.

Step 4: Business Excellence Equation

(Culture X Disciplined Execution) =
Business Excellence

How to incorporate these concepts into your agency

*"I think you are a very **bad man**," said **Dorothy**. "Oh, no, my dear; I'm really a very good **man**, but I'm a very **bad** Wizard, I must admit."*
-— L. Frank Baum, The Wonderful Wizard of Oz.

• **Culture**

In the earlier chapters, I discussed the three different cultures, the "**systems**," "**people**," and the "**competition**" culture. Step 1 and Step 2 are pretty clear, but how do you incorporate step 3? You will have a dominant culture, but you will need to incorporate all three cultures into your agency. How do you get started? Remember, it's not where you start, but it's where you finish. You are an amazing unique individual, but you may be struggling being the wizard in your agency. Celebrate your strengths and work on your challenges one step at a time. It is a journey.

First, if you are not conducting a weekly team meeting and the annual "fall/strategy" meeting, incorporate these into your office as soon as possible. These two components incorporate all three cultures, so they will be the most effective components to implement in your office.

Second, go to www.cultureofagency.com and complete the culture of agency quiz. This will give you a score on each of these cultures. The highest score will be your dominant culture. Were you surprised by this? Probably not. Your vision statement usually reflects your culture. Which culture is your lowest score? This is where you start. Are you doing the three essential components of that culture? If you are not, then pick one of the essential components that you are not doing. Do it consistently for a set amount of time. I can't tell you the exact time frame, because everyone is different. Some agencies can incorporate something new and master this in a month. Some agencies will take six months. Every agency is unique. Don't compare yourself to others; just do your best and improve every day.

For example, if your lowest score was in the "**systems culture**," review the three essential components of the "**systems culture"**. Let's say that you have no written systems for your agency. Pick one system or process (i.e., auto quoting), and write out a system for auto quoting or borrow one from another agent. If you borrow from another agent, make sure it is a system that you and your team can and want to implement in your agency. Then implement this process in your agency until you are doing it consistently. I didn't say perfectly - I said consistently. Design a way of tracking this. Then pick another system or process and start again.

If you are doing the three essential components of that culture, then what culture has the next lowest score? Again, are you doing all three essential components of that culture? If you are not, then pick one component to improve that culture. Do it consistently until it becomes part of your agency.

If after a month, there is no improvement (you won't know this if you are not tracking it), it may be a training issue. Make sure your team feels comfortable with the process. You will have to remind them of the agreed "values" and help them overcome their fears. You may have to ask yourself, "Do I have the right people, and are they in the right positions?"

Do this until you have incorporated all three essential components from the three cultures. Many agencies make the mistake of trying to incorporate too many new systems or processes at once. It becomes overwhelming to the agent and the team. Just do one thing at a time. Agency is a marathon, not a sprint!

Even if your agency has implemented all the essential components of the three cultures, you will still need to revisit them. Every six months, conduct a meeting with your team and see where your agency can improve. I tell this story about how I hired a personal trainer. I needed to lose twenty pounds. Ugghhh, I am still battling these twenty pounds. Anyway, this personal trainer was beautiful. I know that my hubby will read this book. Sorry honey, but yes, he was gorgeous! His body was perfect, but he had a physical fitness goal. His right bicep was about 1 cm larger than his left bicep, so he was doing exercises on his left bicep. He was doing daily workout activities to accomplish his goal. I tell this story, because some agencies need to lose 20 pounds. Maybe some agencies need to lose 100 pounds. Some agencies are beautiful and just need to have their right bicep match their left bicep. It doesn't matter where you start. It only matters where you want to go!

• **Disciplined Execution:**

Culture is the start of a successful agency, but disciplined execution is the multiplier. You can't continue to foster a winning culture without disciplined execution.

You incorporate the **"systems culture"** by creating systems for your office - how to process quotes, how to conduct an appointment, how to set up an appointment, how to ask for a referral, how to pivot to another line of insurance, how to hire and train a new team member, etc. But you won't have success unless you execute these amazing systems.

In my agency, we have daily money-making activities. These are activities that will generate income for the agency. They are pivots, marketing calls, quotes, appointments, and referrals. These are the activities that will generate the results we want to see, the production. For example, we have to exercise and eat well daily in order to generate the results we want to see on the scale. It's the daily activities that create success. You can't cram them in to one day and hope to see the results consistently. You have to perform the activities consistently, to see the consistent results.

Years ago, I decided that it was time to get into shape, and I joined Orange Theory with friends. For three weeks, I went 3-4 times a week. If you have never gone to Orange Theory, they set you up with a heart monitor and based on the readings, you get "splat" points. Your "splat" points are displayed on large monitors all over the gym. The goal for each workout is to get 12 points. The first week, I got 2-3 splat points at each workout. The second week, I got 3-4 splat points. The third week, I got 4-5 points each workout. At this point, I was getting frustrated. I was working hard. In fact, I was running while my girlfriends were walking on the treadmill, but they would get their 12 points. I raised my hand and asked if something was wrong with my heart monitor. I was informed that nothing was wrong. I talked to my husband who told me that I was probably not working out hard enough. <u>Seriously</u> - challenge accepted!

The first day of week four, I pushed myself to the limit. I thought I was going to throw up. At the end of the class, I got 13 splat points, and everyone clapped for me. It was amazing, but I could not walk for a week. In fact, the next day, my husband had to help me out of bed. It was so painful, that I never went back to Orange Theory.

I tell this story, because I feel like many agency owners do this in their agency. They push to their limit for many years, and then they get burned out. Many do this to their team members who get burned out and leave insurance. If I would have continued on my "Orange Theory" path implementing consistent steps forward, I probably would have hit the splat points in 2 -3 months, maybe even quicker. If I had been consistently improving, it could have been a sustainable workout for me. Instead, I didn't want to do the slow consistent work. I wanted immediate results! And, don't we all?

Being accountable is about the daily consistent activities. By doing those, you are constantly improving. Again, even when I reach my goal weight, I will still need to exercise and eat well. These daily practices never go away. It is a lifestyle. Just like this, these activities need to be part of your agency's lifestyle. We are always aiming for progression, not perfection. In the words of Tony Robbins, "*Progress equals happiness.*"

Conclusion

Every agency owner has their own story of how they got into this business. Your team, your location, your client base, and just **You**, makes up your agency. That is why you have your "unique **culture mix."** You just have to find the right mix to reach the success you deserve. It is work, and there are no quick-fixes, but it is probably not any more work than what you are currently doing. In fact, agency will become more fun, because you are implementing the correct culture for **You** and **Your** team. When you get the right mix, you, the "**Wizard of Agency**" will make magic! Your team will be dedicated, intelligent, and talented people who strive to succeed.

Right now, some of you are working in your agency as an additional team member. You are burnt out. Some of you are checked out and neglecting your agency. You are only putting out fires, and you didn't sign up to be a firefighter. Like I said, this is not a quick fix, and you will have to do some work to be the leader of your agency and create this unique culture. You will have to be "open" to change in order to implement changes; but once you do, it will be magic! You will say, "why didn't I do this earlier? It's not that hard." I apologize that all my analogies are fitness related; but heck, it's like starting to run. The first day you may not even be able to run for a minute. But after disciplined execution, running three to four times a week for two months, you can run a 5k easily. It's always hard to start.

Don't get discouraged. It is about progress and not perfection. **You** are a unique, wonderful creation! And, once you find and implement the right culture mix for you and your team, you will have the success you and your team deserve. This takes time, and you as the agency owner must be willing to do some heavy lifting. Be the "**Wizard**" and "**Find the Magic**!"

Acknowledgement

There are so many people to thank. First, I would like to thank my family for all their support, especially my husband, Kerry, who puts up with all my craziness with love and laughter. My family is the guiding light that directs everything I do in life. Even though sometimes my crazy boys, Tyler and Gavin, drive me crazy, they are my everything. My husband, my soul mate, keeps me grounded and always supports my endeavors and adventures.

Second, I want to thank Karen Wilkes, my mentor, and her husband, Darryl Martin. Karen reached out to me when I was a new agent. She knew how hard it is to start an agency and has been a mentor to me throughout the years. Karen, a talented author, also helped me edit this book. Thank you so much for your expertise and guidance. Darryl, an amazing artist, took the concept of my book and created a meaningful visual representation for my book cover, and helped me with all the logistics associated with publishing a book. This book would not have been the same without their guidance.

I also need to thank my amazing team, Daniel, Roxy, Shannon, Lizzy, Catherine, and Surena. They all jumped on and decided to go on this journey with me. I especially need to thank Daniel Shin and Roxanna Rangel. They have been with me almost a decade. They have tolerated me when I was an ineffective agent, and they have grown with me on this path. I can't express my gratitude enough.

I also want to thank all my insurance agent friends. I named a few in this book, but there are too many to list. I have amazing agency friends. To my WDS study group, thank you for all your knowledge and for helping me grow over the past few years. To other agents, I know that I have learned so much from all of you - from systems, to sales, and to leadership. I so appreciate the support and information sharing.

Finally, I want to thank my forum mates from Entrepreneur's Organization. Your experience shares have been extremely valuable both personally and professionally. In addition, I don't know if I would have been brave enough to put this book out into the universe without your support.

Made in the USA
Monee, IL
11 November 2026

68342123R00049